Start TO Finish
Second Series

FROM Goat TO Cheese

LISA OWINGS

 LERNER PUBLICATIONS COMPANY ⟩ Minneapolis

Lerner Publications Company
A division of Lerner Publishing Group, Inc.
241 First Avenue North
Minneapolis, MN 55401 USA

For reading levels and more information, look up this title at www.lernerbooks.com.

Library of Congress Cataloging-in-Publication Data

Cataloging-in-Publication Data for *From Goat to Cheese* is on file at the Library of Congress.
ISBN: 978-1-4677-6023-2 (LB)
ISBN: 978-1-4677-6111-6 (PB)
ISBN: 978-1-4677-6286-1 (EB)

Manufactured in the United States of America
1 – CG – 12/31/14

TABLE OF Contents

Goat Cheese is tasty! How is it made?

First, farmers raise dairy goats.

Goat cheese is made from goats' milk. Farmers raising dairy goats must wait until the goats are old enough to have babies. After a female goat gives birth, she produces milk.

Next, farmers milk the goats.

Farmers milk the female goats about twice a day. Some farmers milk the goats by hand. Others use machines. The farmers store the milk until they are ready to make cheese.

Workers heat the milk.

The first step in making cheese is often to **pasteurize** the milk. Workers gently heat the milk. This gets rid of harmful germs. The process helps make sure the finished cheese is safe to eat.

Then the milk curdles.

The pasteurized milk is poured into large tubs. Workers add **cultures** to the milk. Then they stir in **rennet**. Finally, they leave the milk for twelve hours or more. During this time, the added ingredients help the milk curdle.

Workers separate the curds and whey.

After a solid curd has formed, workers cut it into smaller pieces. They scoop the curds out of the liquid whey and place them in **cheesecloth** or cheese **molds**. These materials allow the extra whey to drain out.

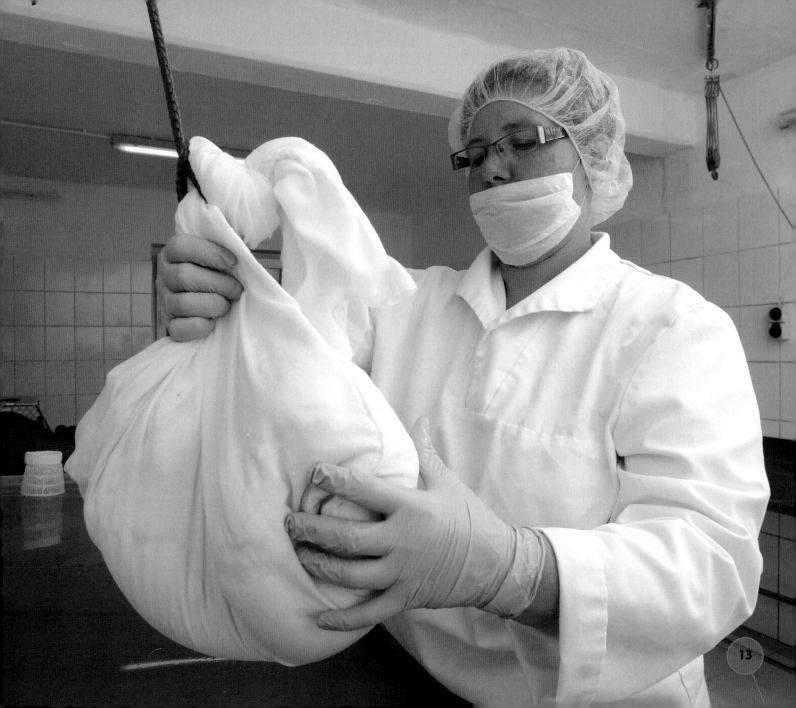

Then they let the cheese ripen.

Next, the cheese is often left to ripen. This can take from several hours to several months. As the cheese ages, it develops the desired flavor and texture.

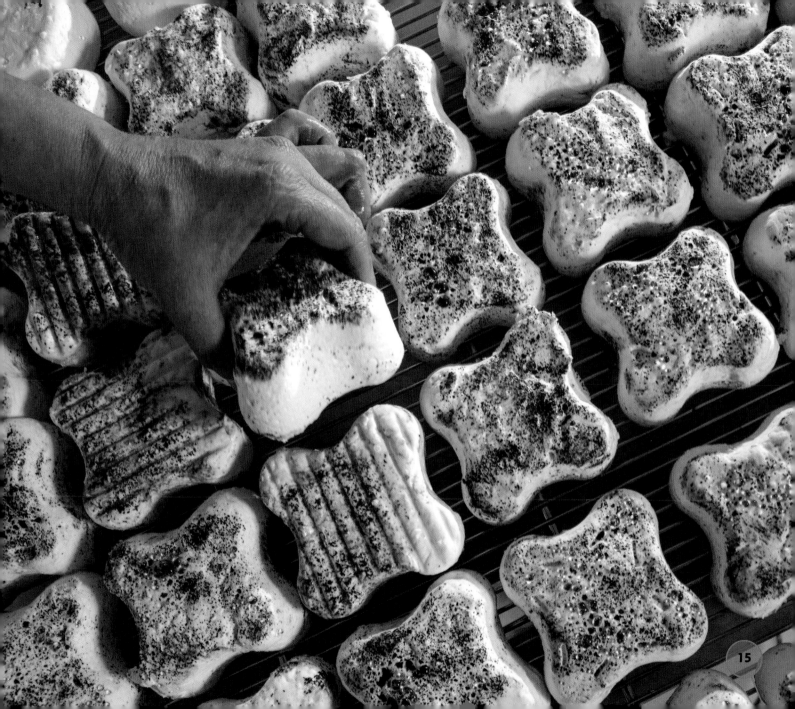

Next, workers salt the cheese.

When the cheese is ready, workers add salt to it. The salt **enhances** the flavor of the cheese. It also helps keep the cheese from spoiling.

Workers shape and package the cheese.

Cheese made in molds already has the perfect shape. Workers shape other cheeses into logs, balls, or discs. Often workers roll the goat cheese in fresh herbs or spices. Then they package it and ship it to stores.

Finally, the cheese is ready to eat!

Goat cheese is healthful and easy to **digest**. There are many varieties of goat cheese, from fresh cheese that is soft and mild to aged cheese that is firm and has a sharper flavor. You can enjoy them all!

Glossary

cheesecloth: thin cotton cloth that easily allows whey to drain out of cheese curds

cultures: special kinds of good bacteria that help turn milk into cheese

curdles: forms lumps called curds

curds: the solid parts of milk that clump together when milk curdles

digest: to break down food so the body can use it

enhances: makes something better

molds: containers that give objects their shape. Cheese molds have holes to allow the whey to drain out.

pasteurize: to heat liquid to a temperature that kills harmful germs

rennet: a substance found in the stomachs of young mammals, usually calves, that is used to curdle milk. Rennet can also be made without animal products.

whey: the liquid part of milk that separates from the solids when milk curdles

Further Information

Cleary, Brian P. *Yogurt and Cheeses and Ice Cream That Pleases: What Is in the Milk Group?* Minneapolis: Millbrook Press, 2011. Learn about all kinds of dairy products and why they are good for you in this book.

FETCH! with Ruff Ruffman: Making Cheese
http://pbskids.org/video/?category=FETCH!%2520with%2520Ruff%2520Ruffman&pid=Hsa_G4e6xVMM2YYn1HuwQ_ITGa9J3T_V
Check out this video to see how fresh cheese is made.

How to Make Great Fresh Mozzarella Cheese
http://www.instructables.com/id/Great-Mozzarella-Cheese/?ALLSTEPS
Want to try making your own cheese? Ask an adult to help you follow this recipe for great-tasting mozzarella.

Mercer, Abbie. *Goats on a Farm.* New York: PowerKids Press, 2010. Read this book to find out more about how goats are raised on farms.

Tuminelly, Nancy. *Let's Cook with Cheese! Delicious & Fun Cheese Dishes Kids Can Make.* Minneapolis: Abdo, 2013. Try the delicious cheese recipes in this book with the help of an adult!

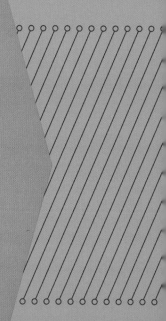

Index

Photo Acknowledgments

The images in this book are used with the permission of:
© Christian Jung/Shutterstock.com, pp. 1,3; © Mark J.
Barrett/Alamy, p. 5; © Monty Rakusen/Cultura Creative
(RF)/Alamy, p. 7; © Javier Larrea/ age fotostock Spain, S.L./
Alamy, p. 9; © SuperStock, p. 11; © Seeberg/Caro/Alamy,
p. 13; © Forget Patrick/Sagaphoto.com/Alamy,
p. 15; © Derek Davis/Portland Press Herald via Getty
Images, p. 17; © Bastian Parschau/Getty Images, p. 19;
© Nitr/Shutterstock.com, p. 21.

Front cover: © Lsantilli/Dreamstime.com.

Main body text set in Arta Std Book 20/26.
Typeface provided by International Typeface Corp.